Publications International, Ltd.

Favorite Brand Name Recipes at www.fbnr.com

Recipe Development: Bev Bennett, Alison Reich and Marcia Kay Stanley.

Pictured on the front cover *(clockwise from top left):* Marshmallow Fudge Sundae Cupcakes *(page 50),* Ice Cream Sandwiches *(page 34),* Miss Pinky the Pig Cupcakes *(page 52)* and Cranberry Gems *(page 24).*

Pictured on the back cover: Sleepover Cake *(page 84).*

ISBN: 1-4127-2434-1

Manufactured in China.

8 7 6 5 4 3 2 1

Microwave Cooking: Microwave ovens vary in wattage. Use the cooking times as guidelines and check for doneness before adding more time.

Contents

Cake Mix Basics

So many occasions, so little time!

Whether you need cookies for a classroom snack, cupcakes for a bake sale or an unforgettable birthday cake, you might not have time for traditional, made-from-scratch baking. But you don't need complicated recipes with lots of ingredients to create beautiful, crowd-pleasing treats. Baking should be easy—and fun!

Cake Mix Fun puts the fun back in baking, with simple recipes and easy-to-follow instructions. Combining cake mix with a few additional ingredients is the best way to create wonderful desserts with minimal time and effort. And unlike scratch baking, where a little mistake might throw off a whole recipe, cake mixes are actually formulated to withstand inconsistencies such as overmixing and pan size discrepancies. So even if you're a baking novice, you're almost guaranteed to succeed.

Cake Mix Confusion

While baking with cake mixes is easy, there are still a few important things to know before you begin. All cake mixes are *not* the same. Make sure you read the recipe carefully to see what kind of cake mix is required, then look closely at your options in the supermarket and check the following:

 **Package size**

Most cake mixes are for two-layer cakes (about 18 ounces) but some are for one-layer cakes (about 9 ounces). The recipe will specify which size to use.

Pudding or no pudding

The majority of the cake mixes available today contain pudding, which is always stated on the package—if the box does not say the mix contains pudding then there is no pudding in the mix. Many of the recipes in this book specify which type of mix to use; if no specific type is given, you can use whichever kind you prefer. (Keep in mind that mixes with pudding should never be used when a recipe contains instant pudding as an ingredient.)

 Oil vs. butter

The directions on cake mix packages list the ingredients you need to add to the mix, usually water, eggs and vegetable oil. Only a few mixes call for butter instead of oil, and these mixes will have the words "butter recipe" somewhere on the package. Using butter results in a slightly different flavor and texture in the final product. Just a few recipes in this book require a butter recipe mix; otherwise you should use the standard mixes that call for oil and are far more prevalent on the supermarket shelves.

Cake Mix Fundamentals

Follow these simple guidelines for successful baking:

• Read the entire recipe before beginning to make sure you have all the necessary ingredients and baking utensils.

• Remove butter and cream cheese from the refrigerator to soften, if necessary.

• Adjust the oven racks and preheat the oven. Check the oven temperature for accuracy with an oven thermometer.

• Use standardized measuring spoons and cups when measuring dry ingredients. Fill the appropriate measuring spoon or cup to overflowing and level it off with a metal spatula or the flat edge of a knife.

• Use a standard glass or plastic measuring cup with calibrations marked on the side when measuring liquid ingredients. Place the cup on a flat surface, fill to the desired mark and check the measurement at eye level.

• Always use the pan size specified in the recipe, and prepare the pan as directed in the recipe or the package directions.

• When substituting glass bakeware in recipes that call for baking pans, reduce the oven temperature by 25°F.

• Follow the recipe directions and baking times. Check for doneness using the test given in the recipe.

Lip-Smackin' Snack Cakes

S'MORE SNACK CAKE

Makes 24 servings

 1 package (18¼ ounces) yellow cake mix, plus ingredients to prepare mix
 1 cup chocolate chunks, divided
1½ cups miniature marshmallows
 1 cup bear-shaped graham crackers (honey or chocolate flavor)

1. Preheat oven to 350°F. Grease 13×9-inch baking pan.

2. Prepare cake mix according to package directions. Spread batter in prepared pan. Sprinkle with ½ cup chocolate chunks.

3. Bake 30 minutes. Remove cake from oven; sprinkle with remaining ½ cup chocolate chunks and marshmallows. Arrange bears evenly over top of cake as shown in photo.

4. Return cake to oven; bake 8 minutes or until marshmallows are golden brown. Cool completely before cutting.

Note: This cake is best served the day it is made.

S'More Snack Cake

TOPSY-TURVY BANANA CRUNCH CAKE

Makes 9 servings

⅓ cup uncooked old-fashioned oats

3 tablespoons packed brown sugar

1 tablespoon all-purpose flour

¼ teaspoon ground cinnamon

2 tablespoons butter

2 tablespoons chopped pecans

1 package (9 ounces) yellow cake mix *without* pudding in the mix

½ cup sour cream

½ cup mashed banana (about 1 medium)

1 egg, lightly beaten

1. Preheat oven to 350°F. Lightly grease 8-inch square baking pan.

2. Combine oats, brown sugar, flour and cinnamon in small bowl. Cut in butter with pastry blender or 2 knives until crumbly. Stir in pecans.

3. Combine cake mix, sour cream, banana and egg in medium bowl. Beat with electric mixer at low speed about 1 minute or until blended. Increase speed to medium; beat 1 to 2 minutes or until smooth. Spoon half of batter into prepared pan; sprinkle with half of oat topping. Top with remaining batter and topping.

4. Bake 25 to 30 minutes or until toothpick inserted into center comes out clean. Cool completely on wire rack.

Lip-Smackin' Snack Cakes

DOUBLE CHOCOLATE CHIP SNACK CAKE

Makes 8 to 10 servings

1 package (18¼ ounces) devil's food cake mix with pudding in the mix, divided
2 eggs
½ cup water
¼ cup vegetable oil
½ teaspoon cinnamon
1 cup semisweet chocolate chips, divided
¼ cup packed brown sugar
2 tablespoons butter, melted
¾ cup white chocolate chips

1. Preheat oven to 350°F. Grease 9-inch round cake pan. Reserve ¾ cup cake mix; set aside.

2. Pour remaining cake mix into large bowl. Add eggs, water, oil and cinnamon; beat with electric mixer at medium speed 2 minutes. Remove ½ cup batter; reserve for another use*. Spread remaining batter in prepared pan; sprinkle with ½ cup chocolate chips.

3. Combine reserved cake mix and brown sugar in medium bowl. Stir in butter and remaining ½ cup semisweet chocolate chips; mix well. Sprinkle mixture over batter in pan.

4. Bake 35 to 40 minutes or until toothpick inserted into center comes out clean and cake springs back when lightly touched.

5. Place white chocolate chips in resealable food storage bag; seal bag. Microwave on HIGH 10 seconds and knead bag gently. Repeat until chips are melted. Cut off ¼ inch from corner of bag with scissors; drizzle chocolate over cake. Cool cake on wire rack before cutting into wedges.

If desired, extra batter can be used for cupcakes: Pour batter into two foil or paper cupcake liners placed on baking sheet; bake at 350°F 20 to 25 minutes or until toothpick inserted into centers comes out clean.

Lip-Smackin' Snack Cakes

CRUNCHY PEACH SNACK CAKE

Makes 9 servings

1 package (9 ounces) yellow cake mix *without* pudding in the mix
1 container (6 ounces) peach-flavor yogurt
1 egg
¼ cup peach all-fruit spread
¾ cup square whole grain oat cereal with cinnamon, slightly crushed
   Whipped cream (optional)

1. Place rack in center of oven; preheat oven to 350°F. Lightly grease 8-inch square baking pan.

2. Beat cake mix, yogurt and egg in medium bowl with electric mixer at low speed about 1 minute or until blended. Increase speed to medium; beat 1 to 2 minutes or until smooth.

3. Spread batter in prepared pan. Drop fruit spread by ½ teaspoonfuls over cake batter. Sprinkle with cereal.

4. Bake about 25 minutes or until toothpick inserted into center of cake comes out clean. Cool on wire rack. Serve with whipped cream, if desired.

TORTOISE SNACK CAKE

Makes 24 servings

1 package (18¼ ounces) devil's food cake mix, plus ingredients to prepare mix
1 cup chopped pecans
1 cup chocolate chips
½ teaspoon vanilla
½ cup prepared caramel sauce

1. Preheat oven to 350°F. Grease 13×9-inch baking pan.

2. Prepare cake mix according to package directions. Stir pecans, chocolate chips and vanilla into batter. Pour into prepared pan. Drizzle ½ cup caramel sauce over batter; swirl caramel into batter with knife.

3. Bake 32 minutes or until cake begins to pull away from sides of pan and toothpick inserted into center comes out clean. Cool to lukewarm on wire rack. Garnish each serving with additional pecans and caramel sauce, if desired.

TAFFY APPLE SNACK CAKE

Makes 9 servings

1 package (18¼ ounces) yellow cake mix with pudding in the mix, divided
2 eggs
¼ cup vegetable oil
¼ cup water
¼ cup packed brown sugar, divided
2 medium apples, peeled and diced
1 cup chopped nuts (optional)
2 tablespoons butter, melted
¼ teaspoon ground cinnamon
½ cup caramel topping

1. Preheat oven to 350°F. Spray 8-inch square baking pan with nonstick cooking spray. Reserve ¾ cup cake mix; set aside.

2. Pour remaining cake mix into large bowl. Add eggs, oil, water and 2 tablespoons brown sugar; beat with electric mixer at medium speed 2 minutes. Stir in apples; spread in prepared pan.

3. Combine reserved cake mix, remaining 2 tablespoons brown sugar, nuts, butter and cinnamon in medium bowl; mix until well blended. Sprinkle over batter. Bake 40 to 45 minutes or until toothpick inserted into center comes out clean.

4. Cool cake in pan on wire rack. Cut into squares; top each serving with about 2 teaspoons caramel topping.

If your brown sugar has dried out, try adding a slice of apple or bread to the box or bag. This will help restore moisture.

CARROT SNACK CAKE

Makes 24 servings

1 package (18¼ ounces) butter recipe yellow cake mix with pudding in the mix, plus ingredients to prepare mix

2 jars (4 ounces each) strained carrot baby food

1½ cups chopped walnuts, divided

1 cup shredded carrots

½ cup golden raisins

1½ teaspoons ground cinnamon

1½ teaspoons vanilla, divided

1 package (8 ounces) cream cheese, softened

Grated peel of 1 lemon

2 teaspoons fresh lemon juice

3 cups powdered sugar

1. Preheat oven to 350°F. Grease 13×9-inch baking pan.

2. Prepare cake mix according to package directions but use only ½ cup water instead of amount directions call for. Stir carrot baby food, 1 cup walnuts, carrots, raisins, cinnamon and ½ teaspoon vanilla into batter. Spread in prepared pan.

3. Bake 40 minutes or until cake begins to pull away from sides of pan and toothpick inserted into center comes out clean. Cool completely in pan on wire rack.

4. Beat cream cheese in large bowl with electric mixer until fluffy. Beat in lemon peel, lemon juice and remaining 1 teaspoon vanilla. Gradually add powdered sugar, scraping down side of bowl occasionally; beat until well blended and smooth. Spread frosting over cooled cake; sprinkle with remaining ½ cup walnuts. Refrigerate 2 hours before cutting.

Cookie Jar Concoctions

CHOCOLATE GINGERSNAPS

Makes about 3 dozen cookies

¾ cup sugar
1 package (18¼ ounces) chocolate cake mix *without* pudding in the mix
1 tablespoon ground ginger
2 eggs
⅓ cup vegetable oil

1. Preheat oven to 350°F. Spray cookie sheets with nonstick cooking spray. Pour sugar into shallow bowl.

2. Combine cake mix and ginger in large bowl. Add eggs and oil; stir until well blended.

3. Shape dough into 1-inch balls, using about 1 tablespoon dough for each cookie. Roll in sugar to coat. Place 2 inches apart on prepared cookie sheets.

4. Bake 10 minutes; transfer to wire racks to cool completely.

CINNAMON CEREAL CRISPIES

Makes about 5 dozen cookies

½ cup granulated sugar

2 teaspoons ground cinnamon, divided

1 package (18¼ ounces) white or yellow cake mix with pudding in the mix

½ cup water

⅓ cup vegetable oil

1 egg

2 cups crisp rice cereal

1 cup cornflakes

1 cup raisins

1 cup chopped nuts (optional)

1. Preheat oven to 350°F. Lightly spray cookie sheets with nonstick cooking spray. Combine sugar and 1 teaspoon cinnamon in small bowl.

2. Beat cake mix, water, oil, egg and remaining 1 teaspoon cinnamon in large bowl with electric mixer at medium speed 1 minute. Gently stir in rice cereal, cornflakes, raisins and nuts until well blended.

3. Drop batter by rounded tablespoonfuls 2 inches apart onto prepared cookie sheets. Sprinkle lightly with cinnamon-sugar mixture.

4. Bake about 15 minutes or until lightly browned. Sprinkle cookies with additional cinnamon-sugar after baking; transfer to wire racks to cool completely.

Cool your cookie sheets completely before placing dough on them to bake another batch. Dough will soften and begin to spread on a hot cookie sheet.

CRANBERRY GEMS

Makes about 5 dozen cookies

⅔ cup dried cranberries or dried cherries
½ cup granulated sugar
3 tablespoons water, divided
1 package (18¼ ounces) white cake mix with pudding in the mix
2 eggs
2 tablespoons vegetable oil
¼ teaspoon almond or vanilla extract
½ cup powdered sugar
1 to 2 teaspoons milk

1. Preheat oven to 350°F. Lightly grease cookie sheets.

2. Combine dried cranberries, granulated sugar and 1 tablespoon water in small microwavable bowl. Microwave on HIGH 1 minute; let cranberries stand 10 minutes before draining.

3. Blend cake mix, eggs, remaining 2 tablespoons water, oil and almond extract in large bowl until smooth. Drop batter by rounded teaspoonfuls 2 inches apart onto prepared cookie sheets. Top each cookie with several cranberries.

4. Bake 10 minutes or until edges are lightly browned. Top each cookie with another one or two cranberries after baking; transfer to wire racks to cool completely.

5. Blend powdered sugar and 1 teaspoon milk in small bowl until smooth. Add additional milk if necessary to reach pourable consistency. Drizzle glaze over cookies with tip of small spoon or fork.

MOON ROCKS

Makes 60 cookies

1 package (18¼ ounces) devil's food or German chocolate cake mix with pudding in the mix

3 eggs

½ cup (1 stick) butter, melted

2 cups slightly crushed (2½-inch) pretzel sticks

1½ cups uncooked old-fashioned oats

1 cup swirled chocolate and white chocolate chips or candy-coated semisweet chocolate baking pieces

1. Preheat oven to 350°F. Blend cake mix, eggs and butter in large bowl. Stir in crushed pretzels, oats and chocolate chips. (Dough will be stiff.)

2. Drop dough by rounded teaspoonfuls about 2 inches apart onto ungreased cookie sheets.

3. Bake 7 to 9 minutes or until set. Let cookies stand on cookie sheets 1 minute; transfer to wire racks to cool completely.

To crush pretzels, place them in a plastic food storage bag, seal the bag and press on them with a rolling pin, a measuring cup or even your hands.

SUNSHINE SANDWICHES

Makes 30 cookies

⅓ cup coarse or granulated sugar
¾ cup (1½ sticks) plus 2 tablespoons butter, softened, divided
1 egg
2 tablespoons grated lemon peel
1 package (18¼ ounces) lemon cake mix with pudding in the mix
¼ cup yellow cornmeal
2 cups sifted powdered sugar
2 to 3 tablespoons lemon juice
2 drops yellow food coloring (optional)

1. Preheat oven to 375°F. Place coarse sugar in shallow bowl.

2. Beat ¾ cup butter in large bowl with electric mixer at medium speed until fluffy. Add egg and lemon peel; beat 30 seconds. Add cake mix, ⅓ at a time, beating at low speed after each addition until combined. Stir in cornmeal. (Dough will be stiff.)

3. Shape dough into 1-inch balls; roll in sugar to coat. Place 2 inches apart on ungreased cookie sheets.

4. Bake 8 to 9 minutes or until bottoms begin to brown. Let cookies stand on cookie sheets 1 minute; transfer to wire racks to cool completely.

5. Meanwhile, beat powdered sugar and remaining 2 tablespoons butter in small bowl with electric mixer at low speed until blended. Gradually add enough lemon juice to reach spreading consistency. Stir in food coloring, if desired.

6. Spread 1 slightly rounded teaspoon frosting on bottom of one cookie. Top with second cookie, bottom side down. Repeat with remaining cookies and frosting. Store covered at room temperature for up to 24 hours or freeze.

GARBAGE PAIL COOKIES

Makes 40 cookies

    1 package (18¼ ounces) white cake mix with pudding in the mix
    ½ cup (1 stick) butter, softened
    2 eggs
    1 teaspoon vanilla
    1 teaspoon ground cinnamon
    ½ cup mini candy-coated chocolate pieces
    ½ cup salted peanuts
    ½ cup peanut butter chips
    1½ cups crushed salted potato chips

1. Preheat oven to 350°F. Lightly grease cookie sheets.

2. Beat half of cake mix, butter, eggs, vanilla and cinnamon in large bowl with electric mixer at medium speed until light. Beat in remaining cake mix until well blended. Stir in candy-coated chocolate pieces, peanuts and peanut butter chips. Stir in potato chips. (Dough will be stiff.)

3. Drop batter by rounded tablespoonfuls 2 inches apart onto prepared cookie sheets.

4. Bake 15 minutes or until golden brown. Let cookies stand on cookie sheets 2 minutes; transfer to wire racks to cool completely.

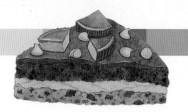

Bar Cookie Bonanza

GRANOLA RAISIN BARS

Makes 15 bars

1 package (18¼ ounces) yellow cake mix with pudding in the mix, divided
½ cup (1 stick) butter, melted, divided
1 egg
4 cups granola cereal with raisins

1. Preheat oven to 350°F. Lightly spray 13×9-inch baking pan with nonstick cooking spray. Reserve ½ cup cake mix; set aside.

2. Combine remaining cake mix, 4 tablespoons melted butter and egg in large bowl; stir until well blended. (Dough will be thick and sticky.) Spoon dough into prepared pan. Cover with plastic wrap and press dough evenly into pan, using plastic wrap to keep hands from sticking to dough.

3. Bake 8 minutes. Meanwhile, combine reserved cake mix, granola cereal and remaining 4 tablespoons melted butter in medium bowl; stir until well blended. Spread mixture evenly over partially baked bars.

4. Return pan to oven; bake 15 to 20 minutes or until edges are lightly browned. Cool completely in pan on wire rack.

Granola Raisin Bars

ICE CREAM SANDWICHES

Makes 8 sandwiches

1 package (18¼ ounces) chocolate cake mix with pudding in the mix
2 eggs
¼ cup warm water
3 tablespoons butter, melted
1 pint vanilla ice cream, softened
  Colored decorating sugar or sprinkles

1. Preheat oven to 350°F. Lightly spray 13×9-inch pan with nonstick cooking spray. Line pan with foil and spray foil.

2. Beat cake mix, eggs, water and melted butter in large bowl with electric mixer until well blended. (Dough will be thick and sticky.) Spoon dough into prepared pan. Cover with plastic wrap and press dough evenly into pan, using plastic wrap to keep hands from sticking to dough. Remove plastic wrap and prick surface all over with fork (about 40 times) to prevent dough from rising too much.

3. Bake 20 minutes or until toothpick inserted into center comes out clean. Cool in pan on wire rack.

4. Cut cookie in half crosswise; remove one half from pan. Spread ice cream evenly over cookie half remaining in pan. Top with second half; use foil in pan to wrap up sandwich.

5. Freeze at least 4 hours. Cut into 8 equal pieces; dip cut ends in sugar or sprinkles. Wrap and freeze sandwiches until ready to serve.

Peppermint Ice Cream Sandwiches: Stir ⅓ cup crushed peppermint candies into vanilla ice cream before assembling. Roll ends of sandwiches in additional crushed peppermint candies to coat.

Tip: If the ice cream is too hard to scoop easily, microwave on HIGH 10 seconds to soften.

PEANUT BUTTER CHEESECAKE BARS

Makes 24 servings

1 package (18¼ ounces) yellow cake mix with pudding in the mix
½ cup (1 stick) butter, softened, cut into small pieces
2 packages (8 ounces each) cream cheese, softened
1 cup chunky peanut butter
3 eggs
1¼ cups sugar
1 cup salted roasted peanuts
Melted chocolate (optional, see Tip)

1. Preheat oven to 325°F. Combine cake mix and butter in large bowl; beat with electric mixer at medium speed just until crumbly. Remove 1 cup mixture. Press remaining mixture evenly into ungreased 13×9-inch baking pan to form crust. Bake 10 minutes; cool on wire rack.

2. Combine cream cheese and peanut butter in large bowl; beat with electric mixer at medium speed until fluffy. Beat in eggs, one at a time, scraping down side of bowl occasionally. Gradually beat in sugar until light. Spoon filling over cooled crust.

3. Combine reserved cake mix mixture and peanuts; spread evenly over filling.

4. Bake 45 minutes or until cake is just set and knife inserted into center comes out clean. Remove from oven; cool at room temperature 30 minutes. Chill at least 2 hours before serving. Drizzle with melted chocolate, if desired.

Tip: For a chocolate drizzle, place ½ cup semisweet chocolate chips in a small resealable food storage bag; seal. Microwave on HIGH (100% power) 1 minute; knead the bag lightly. Microwave on HIGH for additional 30-second intervals until the chips are completely melted, kneading the bag after each interval. Cut off a very tiny corner of the bag; pipe melted chocolate over the cooled cheesecake bars.

BURIED CHERRY BARS

Makes 24 bars

  1 jar (10 ounces) maraschino cherries
  1 package (18¼ ounces) devil's food cake mix *without* pudding in the mix
  1 cup (2 sticks) butter, melted
  1 egg
 ½ teaspoon almond extract
1½ cups semisweet chocolate chips
 ¾ cup sweetened condensed milk
 ½ cup chopped pecans

1. Preheat oven to 350°F. Lightly grease 13×9-inch baking pan. Drain maraschino cherries, reserving 2 tablespoons juice. Cut cherries into quarters.

2. Combine cake mix, butter, egg and almond extract in large bowl; mix well. (Batter will be very thick.) Spread batter in prepared pan. Lightly press cherries into batter.

3. Combine chocolate chips and sweetened condensed milk in small saucepan. Cook over low heat, stirring constantly, until chocolate melts. Stir in reserved cherry juice. Spread chocolate mixture over cherries in pan; sprinkle with pecans.

4. Bake 35 minutes or until almost set in center. Cool completely in pan on wire rack.

Almond extract gives baked goods a distinctive flavor. If your kids don't like it, simply substitute vanilla extract in the recipe.

CHOCOLATE AND OAT TOFFEE BARS

Makes 30 bars

¾ cup (1½ sticks) plus 2 tablespoons butter, softened
1 package (18¼ ounces) yellow cake mix with pudding in the mix
2 cups uncooked quick-cooking oats
¼ cup packed brown sugar
1 egg
½ teaspoon vanilla
1 cup toffee chips
½ cup chopped pecans
⅓ cup semisweet chocolate chips

1. Preheat oven to 350°F. Grease 13×9-inch baking pan.

2. Beat ¾ cup butter in large bowl with electric mixer until creamy. Add cake mix, oats, brown sugar, egg and vanilla; beat 1 minute or until well blended. Stir in toffee chips and pecans. Pat dough into prepared pan.

3. Bake 31 to 35 minutes or until golden brown. Remove from oven and cool completely in pan on wire rack.

4. Melt remaining 2 tablespoons butter and chocolate chips in small saucepan over very low heat. Drizzle warm glaze over bars. Let glaze set 1 hour at room temperature. Cut into bars with sharp knife.

OOEY-GOOEY CARAMEL PEANUT BUTTER BARS

Makes 24 bars

1 package (18¼ ounces) yellow cake mix *without* pudding in the mix
1 cup uncooked quick-cooking oats
⅔ cup creamy peanut butter
1 egg, slightly beaten
2 tablespoons milk
1 package (8 ounces) cream cheese, softened
1 jar (12¼ ounces) caramel ice cream topping
1 cup semisweet chocolate chips

1. Preheat oven to 350°F. Lightly grease 13×9-inch baking pan.

2. Combine cake mix and oats in large bowl. Cut in peanut butter with pastry blender or 2 knives until mixture is crumbly.

3. Blend egg and milk in small bowl. Add to peanut butter mixture; stir just until combined. Reserve 1½ cups mixture. Press remaining peanut butter mixture into prepared pan.

4. Beat cream cheese in small bowl with electric mixer on medium speed until fluffy. Add caramel topping; beat just until combined. Carefully spread over peanut butter layer in pan. Break up reserved peanut butter mixture into small pieces; sprinkle over cream cheese layer. Top with chocolate chips.

5. Bake about 30 minutes or until nearly set in center. Cool completely in pan on wire rack.

CHOCOLATE PEANUT BUTTER CANDY BARS

Makes 24 servings

1 package (18¼ ounces) devil's food or dark chocolate cake mix *without* pudding in the mix

1 can (5 ounces) evaporated milk

⅓ cup butter, melted

½ cup dry-roasted peanuts

4 packages (1½ ounces each) chocolate peanut butter cups, coarsely chopped

1. Preheat oven to 350°F. Lightly grease 13×9-inch baking pan.

2. Combine cake mix, evaporated milk and butter in large bowl; beat with electric mixer at medium speed until well blended. (Dough will be stiff.) Spread ⅔ of dough in prepared pan. Sprinkle with peanuts.

3. Bake 10 minutes; remove from oven and sprinkle with chopped candy.

4. Drop remaining dough by large spoonfuls over candy. Bake 15 to 20 minutes or until set. Cool completely on wire rack.

Chopping peanut butter cups is easier when the candy is partially frozen. Unwrap the candy, place it on a cookie sheet and freeze for one hour.

JAM JAM BARS

Makes 24 bars

1 package (18¼ ounces) yellow or white cake mix with pudding in the mix
½ cup (1 stick) butter, melted
1 cup apricot preserves or raspberry jam
1 package (11 ounces) peanut butter and milk chocolate chips

1. Preheat oven to 350°F. Lightly spray 13×9-inch baking pan with nonstick cooking spray.

2. Pour cake mix into large bowl; stir in melted butter until well blended. (Dough will be lumpy.) Remove ½ cup dough and set aside. Press remaining dough evenly into prepared pan. Spread preserves in thin layer over dough in pan.

3. Place chips in medium bowl. Stir in reserved dough until well mixed. (Dough will remain in small lumps evenly distributed throughout chips.) Sprinkle mixture evenly over preserves.

4. Bake 20 minutes or until lightly browned and bubbling at edges. Cool completely in pan on wire rack.

LEMON CHEESE BARS

Makes 18 bars

1 package (18¼ ounces) white or yellow cake mix with pudding in the mix
2 eggs, divided
⅓ cup vegetable oil
1 package (8 ounces) cream cheese, softened
⅓ cup sugar
1 teaspoon lemon juice

1. Preheat oven to 350°F.

2. Combine cake mix, 1 egg and oil in large bowl; stir until crumbly. Reserve 1 cup crumb mixture. Press remaining crumb mixture into ungreased 13×9-inch baking pan. Bake 15 minutes or until light golden brown.

3. Combine remaining egg, cream cheese, sugar and lemon juice in medium bowl; beat until smooth and well blended. Spread over baked layer. Sprinkle with reserved crumb mixture. Bake 15 minutes or until cream cheese layer is just set. Cool in pan on wire rack.

Crazy for Cupcakes

MINI DOUGHNUT CUPCAKES

Makes about 48 cupcakes

1 cup sugar
1½ teaspoons ground cinnamon
1 package (18¼ ounces) yellow or white cake mix, plus ingredients to prepare mix
1 tablespoon ground nutmeg

1. Preheat oven to 350°F. Grease and flour 24 mini (1¾-inch) muffin pan cups. Combine sugar and cinnamon in small bowl; set aside.

2. Prepare cake mix according to package directions; stir nutmeg into batter. Fill prepared muffin cups ⅔ full.

3. Bake about 12 minutes or until lightly browned and toothpick inserted into centers comes out clean.

4. Remove cupcakes from pans; roll in sugar mixture until completely coated. Serve warm or at room temperature.

Tip: Save any remaining cinnamon-sugar mixture to sprinkle on toast and pancakes.

MARSHMALLOW FUDGE SUNDAE CUPCAKES

Makes 20 cupcakes

1 package (18¼ ounces) chocolate cake mix, plus ingredients to prepare mix
2 packages (4 ounces each) waffle bowls
40 marshmallows
1 jar (8 ounces) hot fudge topping
1¼ cups whipped topping
¼ cup sprinkles
1 jar (10 ounces) maraschino cherries

1. Preheat oven to 350°F. Lightly spray 20 standard (2½-inch) muffin pan cups with nonstick cooking spray.

2. Prepare cake mix according to package directions. Spoon batter into prepared cups, filling ⅔ full.

3. Bake about 20 minutes or until toothpicks inserted into centers come out clean. Cool in pans on wire rack about 10 minutes.

4. Remove cupcakes from pans and place one cupcake in each waffle bowl. Place waffle bowls on baking sheets. Top each cupcake with 2 marshmallows and return to oven for 2 minutes or until marshmallows are slightly softened.

5. Remove lid from fudge topping; heat in microwave on HIGH 10 seconds or until softened. Spoon 2 teaspoons fudge topping over each cupcake. Top with 1 tablespoon whipped topping, sprinkles and cherry.

MISS PINKY THE PIG CUPCAKES

Makes 24 cupcakes

2 jars (10 ounces each) maraschino cherries, well drained
1 package (18¼ ounces) white cake mix *without* pudding in the mix
1 cup sour cream
½ cup vegetable oil
¼ cup water
3 egg whites
½ teaspoon almond extract
Red food coloring
1 container (16 ounces) cream cheese frosting
48 small gum drops
Mini candy-coated chocolate pieces, mini chocolate chips, white decorating icing and colored sugar

1. Preheat oven to 350°F. Line 24 standard (2½-inch) muffin pan cups with paper liners. Spray 24 mini (1¾-inch) muffin pan cups with nonstick cooking spray. Pat cherries dry with paper towels. Place in food processor; process 4 to 5 seconds or until finely chopped.

2. Beat cake mix, sour cream, oil, water, egg whites and almond extract in large bowl with electric mixer at low speed about 1 minute or until blended. Increase speed to medium; beat 1 to 2 minutes or until smooth. Stir in cherries.

3. Spoon about 2 slightly rounded tablespoons batter into prepared standard muffin cups, filling each about ½ full. (Cups will be slightly less full than normal.) Spoon remaining batter into mini muffin cups, filling each about ⅓ full.

4. Bake standard cupcakes 14 to 18 minutes and mini cupcakes 7 to 9 minutes or until toothpick inserted into centers comes out clean. Cool cupcakes in pans on wire racks 5 minutes; remove from pans and cool completely on wire racks. Remove paper liners from larger cupcakes.

5. Add food coloring to frosting, a few drops at a time, until desired color is reached. Frost tops of larger cupcakes with pink frosting. Gently press small cupcake onto one side of each larger cupcake top. Frost tops and sides of small cupcakes.

6. Place gumdrops between two layers of waxed paper. Flatten to ⅛-inch thickness with rolling pin; cut out triangles. Arrange gumdrops on cupcakes for ears; complete faces with candy-coated chocolate pieces, chocolate chips, white icing and colored sugar.

TROPICAL LUAU CUPCAKES

Makes 30 cupcakes

2 cans (8 ounces each) crushed pineapple in juice
1 package (18¼ ounces) yellow cake mix *without* pudding in the mix
1 package (4-serving size) banana cream-flavor instant pudding and pie filling mix
4 eggs
⅓ cup vegetable oil
¼ teaspoon ground nutmeg
1 can (12 ounces) whipped vanilla frosting
¾ cup flaked coconut, toasted
3 to 4 medium kiwi
30 (2½-inch) pretzel sticks

1. Preheat oven to 350°F. Line 30 standard (2½-inch) muffin pan cups with paper liners. Drain pineapple, reserving juice. Set pineapple aside.

2. Beat reserved pineapple juice, cake mix, pudding mix, eggs, oil and nutmeg in large bowl with electric mixer at low speed 1 minute or until blended. Increase speed to medium; beat 1 to 2 minutes or until smooth. Fold in pineapple. Fill muffin cups ⅔ full.

3. Bake about 20 minutes or until toothpick inserted into centers comes out clean. Cool cupcakes in pans on wire racks 5 minutes; remove from pans and cool completely on wire racks.

4. Frost tops of cupcakes with frosting; sprinkle with coconut. For palm trees*, peel kiwi and cut into ⅛-inch-thick slices. Create palm fronds by cutting each slice at ⅜-inch intervals, cutting from outside edge toward center. (Leave about ¾- to 1-inch circle uncut in center of each slice). For palm tree trunk, push pretzel stick into, but not through, center of each kiwi slice. Push other end of pretzel into top of each cupcake.

Palm tree decorations can be made up to 1 hour before serving.

Tip: To toast coconut, spread evenly on ungreased baking sheet; bake in preheated 350°F oven 4 to 6 minutes or until light golden brown, stirring frequently.

Crazy for Cupcakes

CUBCAKES

Makes 24 cupcakes

1 package (18¼ ounces) chocolate cake mix, plus ingredients to prepare mix
1 container (16 ounces) chocolate frosting
1 package (5 ounces) chocolate nonpareil candies
72 red cinnamon candies
   Chocolate sprinkles
   Black decorating gel

1. Line 24 standard (2½-inch) muffin pan cups with paper liners or spray with nonstick cooking spray.

2. Prepare cake mix and bake in prepared pans according to package directions. Cool cupcakes in pans on wire racks 15 minutes; remove from pans and cool completely on wire racks.

3. Frost cooled cupcakes with chocolate frosting. Use nonpareils to create ears and muzzle. Add cinnamon candies for eyes and noses. Decorate with chocolate sprinkles for fur. Use decorating gel to place dots on eyes and create mouth.

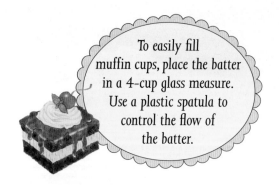

To easily fill muffin cups, place the batter in a 4-cup glass measure. Use a plastic spatula to control the flow of the batter.

DOODLE BUG CUPCAKES

Makes 24 cupcakes

1 package (18¼ ounces) white cake mix *without* pudding in the mix
1 cup sour cream
3 eggs
⅓ cup vegetable oil
⅓ cup water
1 teaspoon vanilla
1½ cups prepared cream cheese frosting
   Red, yellow, blue and green food coloring
   Red licorice strings, cut into 2-inch pieces
   Assorted round decorating candies

1. Preheat oven to 350°F. Line 24 standard (2½-inch) muffin pan cups with paper liners.

2. Beat cake mix, sour cream, eggs, oil, water and vanilla in large bowl with electric mixer at low speed about 1 minute or until blended. Increase speed to medium; beat 1 to 2 minutes or until smooth.

3. Fill muffin cups about ⅔ full. Bake about 20 minutes or until toothpick inserted into centers comes out clean.

4. Cool cupcakes in pans on wire racks 5 minutes; remove from pans and cool completely on wire racks.

5. Divide frosting evenly between 4 small bowls. Add food coloring to each bowl, one drop at a time, to reach desired colors; stir each frosting until well blended. Frost tops of cupcakes.

6. Use toothpick or wooden skewer to make three small holes on opposite sides of each cupcake. Insert licorice piece into each hole for legs. Decorate tops of cupcakes with assorted candies.

LEMON-UP CAKES

Makes 24 cupcakes

1 package (18¼ ounces) butter recipe white cake mix with pudding in the mix, plus ingredients to prepare mix

½ cup fresh lemon juice, divided (2 large lemons)

Grated peel of 2 lemons, divided

½ cup (1 stick) butter, softened

3½ cups powdered sugar

Yellow food coloring

1 package (9½ ounces) lemon-shaped hard candies, coarsely crushed

1. Preheat oven to 350°F. Line 24 standard (2½-inch) muffin pan cups with paper liners.

2. Prepare cake mix according to package directions but use ¼ cup less water than directions call for. Stir in ¼ cup lemon juice and half of grated lemon peel. Fill muffin cups evenly with batter.

3. Bake 23 minutes or until light golden brown and toothpick inserted into centers comes out clean. Cool cupcakes in pans on wire racks 5 minutes; remove from pans and cool completely on wire racks.

4. Beat butter in large bowl with electric mixer at medium speed until creamy. Gradually add powdered sugar to form stiff mixture. Add remaining ¼ cup lemon juice, lemon peel and several drops food coloring; beat at high speed until frosting is light and fluffy.

5. Generously frost cupcakes. Sprinkle crushed candies over frosting.

BUTTERFLY CUPCAKES

Makes 24 cupcakes

1 package (18¼ ounces) cake mix, any flavor, plus ingredients to prepare mix
1 container (16 ounces) white frosting
    Blue and green food coloring
    Assorted candies and colored sugar
    Red licorice ropes, cut into 4-inch pieces

1. Preheat oven to 350°F. Lightly spray 24 standard (2½-inch) muffin pan cups with nonstick cooking spray.

2. Prepare cake mix according to package directions. Spoon batter into prepared muffin cups, filling ⅔ full.

3. Bake about 20 minutes or until toothpicks inserted into centers come out clean. Cool cupcakes in pans on wire racks about 10 minutes; remove from pans and cool completely on wire racks.

4. Divide frosting equally between 2 small bowls. Add food coloring to each bowl, one drop at a time, to reach desired colors; stir each frosting until well blended.

5. Cut cupcakes in half. Place cupcake halves together, cut sides out, to resemble butterfly wings. Frost with desired colors; decorate with candies and colored sugar as desired. Snip each end of licorice rope pieces to form antennae; place in center of each cupcake.

PEANUT BUTTER & MILK CHOCOLATE CUPCAKES

Makes 24 cupcakes

1 package (18¼ ounces) butter recipe yellow cake mix with pudding in the mix, plus ingredients to prepare mix

½ cup creamy peanut butter

2 bars (3½ ounces each) good-quality milk chocolate, broken into small pieces

¼ cup (½ stick) butter, cut into small chunks

¼ cup heavy cream

Dash salt

Peanut butter chips (optional)

1. Preheat oven to 350°F. Line 24 standard (2½-inch) muffin pan cups with paper liners.

2. Prepare cake mix according to package directions with ½ cup peanut butter and ¼ cup butter (instead of ½ cup butter called for in directions). Fill muffin cups evenly with batter.

3. Bake 24 to 26 minutes or until light golden brown and toothpick inserted into centers comes out clean. Cool cupcakes in pans on wire racks 5 minutes; remove from pans and cool completely on wire racks.

4. Combine chocolate, butter, cream and salt in small, heavy saucepan. Heat over very low heat, stirring constantly, just until butter and chocolate melt. Mixture should be tepid, not hot. Immediately spoon about 1 tablespoon chocolate glaze over each cupcake, spreading to cover top. Sprinkle with peanut butter chips, if desired.

PUPCAKES

Makes 24 cupcakes

1 package (18¼ ounces) chocolate cake mix, plus ingredients to prepare mix
½ cup (1 stick) butter, softened
4 cups powdered sugar
¼ to ½ cup half-and-half or milk
 Red and yellow fruit roll-ups
 Assorted colored jelly beans and candy-coated chocolate pieces

1. Preheat oven to 350°F. Line 24 standard (2½-inch) muffin pan cups with paper liners.

2. Prepare cake mix and bake in prepared pans according to package directions. Cool cupcakes in pans on wire racks 15 minutes; remove from pans and cool completely on wire racks.

3. Beat butter in large bowl with electric mixer until creamy. Gradually add powdered sugar to form very stiff frosting, scraping down side of bowl occasionally. Gradually add half-and-half until frosting is of desired consistency.

4. Generously frost tops of cupcakes.

5. Cut out ear and tongue shapes from fruit roll-ups with scissors; arrange on cupcakes, pressing into frosting as shown in photo. Add candies to create eyes and noses.

For a smooth, lump-free frosting, always sift powdered sugar before using it (but sift it after measuring).

Super Cool Cakes

BIG PURPLE PURSE

Makes 8 to 10 servings

1 package (18¼ ounces) cake mix, any flavor, plus ingredients to prepare mix
1 container (16 ounces) white frosting
   Red and blue food coloring
1 piece red licorice rope
1 white chocolate-coated pretzel
   Round sugar-coated colored candies
   Candy lipstick, necklace and ring (optional)

1. Preheat oven to 350°F. Prepare and bake cake mix according to package directions in two 9-inch round cake pans. Cool in pans on wire racks 10 minutes; remove from pans and cool completely on wire racks. Reserve one cake layer for another use.

2. Add 4 drops of each food coloring to frosting; mix well. Add additional food coloring, one drop at a time, to reach desired shade of purple.

3. Spread about ½ cup frosting over top of cake layer. Cut cake in half; press frosted sides together to form half circle. Place cake, flat side down, on serving plate.

4. Spread frosting over top and sides of cake. Cut licorice rope in half; press ends into top of cake to form purse handle. Add pretzel for clasp. Gently press round candies into sides of cake. Arrange candy lipstick, necklace and ring around cake, if desired.

PB & J SANDWICH CAKE

Makes 12 servings

1 package (18¼ ounces) white cake mix, plus ingredients to prepare mix
¾ cup powdered sugar
5 tablespoons peanut butter
2 to 3 tablespoons heavy cream or milk
1 tablespoon butter, softened
½ cup strawberry or grape jam

1. Preheat oven to 350°F. Grease two 8-inch square baking pans. Prepare cake mix according to package directions. Spread batter in prepared pans.

2. Bake 30 minutes or until toothpick inserted into center comes out clean. Cool in pans on wire racks 30 minutes; remove from pans and cool completely on wire racks.

3. Carefully slice off browned tops of both cakes to create flat, even layers. Place 1 layer on serving plate, cut side up.

4. Beat powdered sugar, peanut butter, 2 tablespoons cream and butter with electric mixer at medium speed until light and creamy. Add remaining 1 tablespoon cream if necessary to reach spreading consistency. Gently spread filling over cut side of cake layer on serving plate. Spread jam over peanut butter filling. Top with second cake layer, cut side up.

5. Cut cake in half diagonally to resemble sandwich. To serve, cut into thin slices across the diagonal using serrated knife.

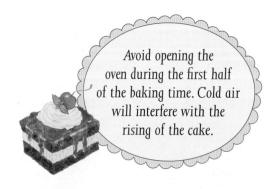

Avoid opening the oven during the first half of the baking time. Cold air will interfere with the rising of the cake.

POLKA DOT CAKE

Makes 16 servings

1 package (18¼ ounces) chocolate cake mix, plus ingredients to prepare mix
¾ cup white chocolate chips
2 bars (3½ ounces each) good-quality bittersweet or semisweet chocolate, broken into small pieces
¼ cup (½ stick) butter, cut into small chunks
¼ cup heavy cream
1 tablespoon powdered sugar
Dash salt
¼ cup small chocolate nonpareil candies

1. Preheat oven to 350°F. Generously spray 12-cup bundt pan with nonstick cooking spray.

2. Prepare cake mix according to package directions. Pour batter into prepared pan; sprinkle with chips.

3. Bake 40 minutes or until toothpick inserted near center comes out clean. Cool cake in pan on wire rack 30 minutes; invert cake onto wire rack and cool completely. Place sheet of waxed paper under wire rack.

4. Combine chocolate, butter, cream, powdered sugar and salt in small, heavy saucepan. Heat over very low heat, stirring constantly, just until butter and chocolate melt. Mixture should be tepid, not hot. Immediately spoon chocolate glaze over cake, spreading to cover side as well as top. Scoop up any glaze from waxed paper and spoon over cake.

5. Arrange nonpareil candies over glaze. Let glaze set about 2 hours at room temperature. Do not refrigerate.

PRETTY PACKAGE CAKE
Makes 12 to 16 servings

CAKE
  1 package (18¼ ounces) lemon cake mix, plus ingredients to prepare mix
  1 container (16 ounces) lemon frosting

RIBBON
  2 cups powdered sugar, sifted
  1 cup marshmallow creme
  Red food coloring

COOKIE GARNISH (OPTIONAL)
  1 package (18 ounces) refrigerated sugar cookie dough
  Colored decorating icings

1. Prepare and bake cake mix according to package directions in two 8-inch square baking pans. Cool completely in pans on wire racks. Remove from pans; fill and frost cake layers with lemon frosting.

2. For ribbon, combine powdered sugar and marshmallow creme in medium bowl; stir until blended. Knead by hand until mixture comes together into stiff, workable dough. (Sprinkle sifted powdered sugar on hands often to keep dough from sticking.) Knead in 2 or 3 drops food coloring until desired color is reached. Roll dough with rolling pin to ¼-inch thickness, sprinkling with sifted powdered sugar as necessary to keep dough from sticking. Cut dough into 1½-inch-wide strips. Place strips over frosted cake to form ribbon and bow; trim ends.

3. For cookie garnish, prepare and bake 2-inch round cookies according to cookie dough package directions. Cool on wire rack. Pipe flowers onto cooled cookies in assorted colors using decorating icings. Garnish cake with cookies.

Tip: This great all-occasion cake can be easily customized for any celebration. Simply frost with appropriate colors and decorate the cookies to match the theme.

BEAUTIFUL BUTTERFLIES

Makes 6 butterflies (2 servings each)

1 package (18¼ ounces) yellow cake mix with pudding in the mix, plus ingredients
    to prepare mix
6 cups powdered sugar
¾ cup (1½ sticks) butter, softened
¾ cup milk or half-and-half
¼ teaspoon salt
    Blue and green food coloring
    Colored candies and mini candy-coated chocolate pieces
    Red licorice string, cut into 1-inch pieces

1. Preheat oven to 350°F. Prepare and bake cake mix according to package directions in 12-cup bundt pan. Cool cake in pan on wire rack 15 minutes; invert onto wire rack and cool completely.

2. Beat powdered sugar, butter, milk and salt in large bowl with electric mixer until light and creamy. Divide frosting between 2 bowls. Tint 1 bowl blue and 1 bowl green (or use only one color, if desired).

3. Cut cake into 4 quarters; cut each quarter into 6 slices to create 24 slices. Cut thin strip from inside of 12 cake slices.

4. For each butterfly, arrange 2 cake strips vertically in center of plate for body. Spread with tinted frosting. Place one trimmed cake slice on each side of body. Place one larger cake slice on each side of body next to small slices as shown in photo. Repeat with remaining cake strips and slices.

5. Decorate with tinted frosting and candies as desired. Arrange 2 pieces licorice at top of each butterfly body for antennae.

LEMON-ORANGE PARTY CAKE

Makes 20 servings

1 package (18¼ ounces) yellow cake mix with pudding in the mix
1¼ cups plus 5 tablespoons orange juice, divided
3 eggs
⅓ cup vegetable oil
2 tablespoons grated orange peel
5½ cups sifted powdered sugar, divided
⅓ cup lemon juice
⅓ cup butter, softened
Multi-colored sprinkles
20 jellied orange or lemon slices

1. Preheat oven to 350°F. Lightly grease 13×9-inch baking pan.

2. Beat cake mix, 1¼ cups orange juice, eggs, oil and orange peel in large bowl with electric mixer at low speed about 1 minute or until blended. Increase speed to medium; beat 1 to 2 minutes or until smooth. Spread in prepared pan.

3. Bake 33 to 38 minutes or until toothpick inserted into center comes out clean. Meanwhile, combine 1 cup powdered sugar and lemon juice in small bowl; stir until smooth.

4. Pierce top of warm cake generously with large fork or wooden skewer (about ½-inch intervals). Slowly drizzle lemon glaze over warm cake. Cool completely.

5. Beat remaining 4½ cups powdered sugar and butter in large bowl with electric mixer on low speed until combined. Beat in enough of remaining orange juice to reach spreading consistency. Gently spread frosting over cooled cake. Decorate top of cake with sprinkles and candied fruit slices.

PONIES IN THE MEADOW

Makes 9 to 12 servings

1 package (18¼ ounces) cake mix, any flavor, plus ingredients to prepare mix
1 cup flaked coconut
   Green food coloring
1 container (16 ounces) white frosting
   Pretzel sticks
2 small plastic ponies

1. Preheat oven to 350°F. Prepare and bake cake mix according to package directions in two 8-inch square baking pans. Cool in pans on wire racks 10 minutes; remove from pans and cool completely on wire racks.

2. Place coconut in small bowl. Add 4 drops green food coloring; stir until well blended. Adjust color with additional drops of food coloring, if necessary.

3. Tint frosting to desired shade of green with food coloring. Place 1 cake layer on serving plate; spread evenly with ½ cup frosting. Top with second cake layer; frost top and sides of cake with remaining frosting. Scatter coconut over top of cake.

4. Stand pretzel sticks around edges of cake to create fence; arrange ponies as desired.

Tip: Additional decorations can be added to the cake, if desired. Arrange candy rocks or brown jelly beans to create a path. Use the star tip on red or yellow decorating icing to create flowers in the meadow.

HIDDEN SURPRISE CAKE

Makes 12 servings

1 package (16 ounces) angel food cake mix, plus ingredients to prepare mix
1½ to 2 pints chocolate ice cream, softened
2 cups heavy cream, well chilled
¼ cup unsweetened cocoa powder
6 tablespoons powdered sugar
2 to 4 tablespoons mini chocolate chips (optional)

1. Prepare, bake and cool angel food cake according to package directions.

2. Place cake on work surface. Using serrated knife, cut horizontally across cake 1 inch from top. Remove top of cake; set aside.

3. Scoop out inside of cake with hands, leaving 1 inch shell on side and bottom. (Be careful not to tear through cake.) Spoon ice cream into cake, packing down. Cover with cake top.

4. Beat cream and cocoa in large bowl with electric mixer at medium speed until slightly thickened. Gradually beat in powdered sugar at high speed until stiff peaks form. Cover top and side of cake with chocolate whipped cream. Sprinkle with chocolate chips, if desired. Serve immediately.

Note: The cake can be prepared and filled, without frosting, up to one week in advance. Wrap in heavy-duty foil and store in the freezer. Remove 15 minutes before frosting. Serve immediately after frosting.

For best results when beating heavy cream, chill the cream, bowl and beaters first. Use a bowl that is deep enough to allow the cream to double in volume.

SLEEPOVER CAKE

Makes 12 servings

1 package (18¼ ounces) cake mix, any flavor, plus ingredients to prepare mix
1 container (16 ounces) white frosting
   Red food coloring
2 long cream-filled snack cakes
   Decorative sugar sprinkles
4 marshmallows
   Red and yellow decorating icing
4 chocolate peanut butter cups (milk or white chocolate)
   Red, black or brown licorice strips (optional)
2 packages (6 feet each) bubble gum tape (pink or green)
   Bear-shaped graham crackers

1. Preheat oven to 350°F. Prepare and bake cake mix according to package directions in 13×9-inch pan. Cool cake in pan on wire rack 10 minutes; remove from pan and cool completely on wire rack.

2. Tint frosting with food coloring to desired shade of pink. Place cake on serving platter; frost top and sides with pink frosting.

3. Cut snack cakes in half lengthwise. Arrange snack cakes, cut sides down, on top of frosted cake. Smooth frosting over snack cakes; sprinkle with decorative sugar sprinkles.

4. Flatten marshmallows by pressing down firmly with palm of hand. Arrange marshmallows at top of snack cakes to create pillows. Use decorating icing to create eyes and lips on peanut butter cups. Add licorice strips for hair, if desired. Place decorated peanut butter cups on marshmallow pillows.

5. Unwind bubble gum tape; arrange across cake at edge of peanut butter cups to form edge of blanket. Arrange second bubble gum tape around base of cake. Tuck bear-shaped graham crackers around blanket.

CANDY BAR CAKE

Makes 12 servings

1 package (18¼ ounces) devil's food cake mix *without* pudding in the mix
1 cup sour cream
4 eggs
⅓ cup vegetable oil
¼ cup water
3 containers (16 ounces each) white frosting
1 bar (2.1 ounces) chocolate-covered crispy peanut butter candy, chopped
1 bar (2.07 ounces) chocolate-covered peanut, caramel and nougat candy, chopped
1 bar (1.4 ounces) chocolate-covered toffee candy, chopped
4 bars (1.55 ounces each) milk chocolate

1. Preheat oven to 350°F. Grease and flour two 9-inch round baking pans.

2. Beat cake mix, sour cream, eggs, oil and water in large bowl with electric mixer at low speed about 1 minute or until blended. Increase speed to medium; beat 1 to 2 minutes or until smooth. Spread batter in prepared pans.

3. Bake 30 to 35 minutes or until toothpick inserted into center comes out clean. Cool in pans on wire racks 10 minutes; remove from pans and cool completely on wire racks.

4. Cut each cake layer in half horizontally. Place 1 cake layer on serving plate. Spread generously with frosting. Sprinkle with 1 chopped candy bar. Repeat with 2 more cake layers, additional frosting and remaining 2 chopped candy bars. Top with remaining cake layer; frost top of cake with remaining frosting.

5. Break milk chocolate bars into pieces along score lines. Stand chocolate pieces in frosting around outside edge of cake as shown in photo.

PEPPERMINT MOUNTAIN RANGE

Makes 16 servings

1 package (18¼ ounces) white or yellow cake mix *without* pudding in the mix
1 package (4-serving size) vanilla instant pudding & pie filling mix
1 cup sour cream
4 eggs
½ cup vegetable oil
⅓ cup water
¾ teaspoon peppermint extract
  Red food coloring
1 cup mini chocolate chips
2 cups sifted powdered sugar
2 to 3 tablespoons milk
½ cup crushed peppermint candies (about 12 round candies)

1. Preheat oven to 350°F. Grease and flour 12-cup bundt pan.

2. Beat cake mix, pudding mix, sour cream, eggs, oil and water in large bowl with electric mixer at low speed about 1 minute or until blended. Increase speed to medium; beat 1 to 2 minutes or until smooth.

3. Combine 1½ cups batter, peppermint extract and 16 drops red food coloring in small bowl; mix well. Stir chocolate chips into remaining batter. Spread half of chocolate chip batter in prepared pan. Spoon peppermint batter on top. Spread remaining chocolate chip batter over peppermint batter.

4. Bake 50 to 60 minutes or until toothpick inserted near center comes out clean. Cool in pan on wire rack 20 minutes; invert cake onto wire rack and cool completely.

5. Blend powdered sugar and 2 tablespoons milk in small bowl until smooth. Add remaining 1 tablespoon milk if necessary to reach drizzling consistency. Drizzle glaze over cooled cake. Sprinkle with crushed candies.

BUCKET OF SAND CAKE

Makes 10 servings

1 package (18¼ ounces) banana or butter pecan cake mix , plus ingredients to prepare mix

½ teaspoon ground cinnamon

¼ teaspoon ground nutmeg

1 package (6-serving size) instant butterscotch-flavor pudding mix, plus ingredients to prepare mix

Clean plastic beach pail and shovel

1½ cups graham cracker or shortbread cookie crumbs, divided

Gummy fish and octopus, starfish and seashell candies, green string candy and mini chocolate chips

1. Preheat oven to 350°F. Prepare and bake cake mix according to package directions in two 9-inch round cake pans, stirring cinnamon and nutmeg into batter. Cool in pans on wire racks 10 minutes; remove from pans and cool completely on wire racks.

2. Meanwhile, prepare pudding mix according to package directions.

3. Cut 1 cake layer into 1-inch slices; arrange about ⅓ of slices in bottom of pail. Spoon ⅓ of pudding over cake slices; top with ⅓ of cake slices. Repeat layers with ⅓ of pudding and remaining cake slices. Sprinkle with 1 cup graham cracker crumbs. Place shovel in cake and decorate with gummy fish and other candies as desired.

4. Cut second cake layer in half horizontally. Place one half, cut side up, on serving plate. Place pail on top of cake layer as shown in photo. Break remaining cake layer into chunks; arrange around base of pail. Spoon remaining pudding over cake chunks; sprinkle remaining ½ cup graham cracker crumbs over pudding. Decorate with candies as desired. To serve, use shovel to spoon cake onto plates.

FLOWER POWER STRAWBERRY CAKE

Makes 15 servings

1 package (18¼ ounces) white cake mix *without* pudding in the mix
2 containers (6 ounces each) strawberry-flavor yogurt
4 eggs
⅓ cup vegetable oil
1 package (4-serving size) strawberry-flavor gelatin
1 container (8 ounces) frozen whipped topping, thawed, divided
12 to 13 medium strawberries
Yellow food coloring

1. Preheat oven to 350°F. Lightly grease 13×9-inch baking pan.

2. Beat cake mix, yogurt, eggs, oil and gelatin in large bowl with electric mixer at low speed about 1 minute or until blended. Increase speed to medium; beat 1 to 2 minutes or until smooth. Spread batter in prepared pan.

3. Bake 38 to 43 minutes or until toothpick inserted into center comes out clean. Cool completely in pan on wire rack.

4. Reserve ½ cup whipped topping. Spread remaining topping over cooled cake. Cut each strawberry lengthwise into 6 wedges. Use strawberry wedges to create 15 flowers on top of cake. For each flower, place 5 strawberry wedges, pointed end towards center, to create flower petals as shown in photo.

5. Tint reserved whipped topping with 6 to 8 drops yellow food coloring. Place tinted topping in resealable food storage bag; cut off ⅛ inch from corner of bag. Pipe yellow whipped topping into center of each flower. Serve cake immediately or loosely cover and refrigerate for up to 24 hours.

Index

METRIC CONVERSION CHART

VOLUME MEASUREMENTS (dry)

1/8 teaspoon = 0.5 mL
1/4 teaspoon = 1 mL
1/2 teaspoon = 2 mL
3/4 teaspoon = 4 mL
1 teaspoon = 5 mL
1 tablespoon = 15 mL
2 tablespoons = 30 mL
1/4 cup = 60 mL
1/3 cup = 75 mL
1/2 cup = 125 mL
2/3 cup = 150 mL
3/4 cup = 175 mL
1 cup = 250 mL
2 cups = 1 pint = 500 mL
3 cups = 750 mL
4 cups = 1 quart = 1 L

VOLUME MEASUREMENTS (fluid)

1 fluid ounce (2 tablespoons) = 30 mL
4 fluid ounces (1/2 cup) = 125 mL
8 fluid ounces (1 cup) = 250 mL
12 fluid ounces (1 1/2 cups) = 375 mL
16 fluid ounces (2 cups) = 500 mL

WEIGHTS (mass)

1/2 ounce = 15 g
1 ounce = 30 g
3 ounces = 90 g
4 ounces = 120 g
8 ounces = 225 g
10 ounces = 285 g
12 ounces = 360 g
16 ounces = 1 pound = 450 g

DIMENSIONS

1/16 inch = 2 mm
1/8 inch = 3 mm
1/4 inch = 6 mm
1/2 inch = 1.5 cm
3/4 inch = 2 cm
1 inch = 2.5 cm

OVEN TEMPERATURES

250°F = 120°C
275°F = 140°C
300°F = 150°C
325°F = 160°C
350°F = 180°C
375°F = 190°C
400°F = 200°C
425°F = 220°C
450°F = 230°C

BAKING PAN SIZES

Utensil	Size in Inches/Quarts	Metric Volume	Size in Centimeters
Baking or Cake Pan (square or rectangular)	8×8×2	2 L	20×20×5
	9×9×2	2.5 L	23×23×5
	12×8×2	3 L	30×20×5
	13×9×2	3.5 L	33×23×5
Loaf Pan	8×4×3	1.5 L	20×10×7
	9×5×3	2 L	23×13×7
Round Layer Cake Pan	8×1½	1.2 L	20×4
	9×1½	1.5 L	23×4
Pie Plate	8×1¼	750 mL	20×3
	9×1¼	1 L	23×3
Baking Dish or Casserole	1 quart	1 L	—
	1½ quart	1.5 L	—
	2 quart	2 L	—